A Power Governments Cannot Suppress (City Lights Books, 2007).

Original Zinn: Conversations on History and Politics, with David Barsamian (HarperCollins/ Perennial, 2006).

A People's History of the United States: 1492–Present, updated ed. (HarperCollins/Perennial, 2005).

The People Speak: American Voices, Some Famous, Some Little Known (HarperCollins/Perennial, 2006).

Voices of a People's History of the United States, with Anthony Arnove (Seven Stories Press, 2004).

Artists in Times of War (Seven Stories Press/Open Media Series, 2003).

Passionate Declarations: Essays on War and Justice (Harper/Perennial, 2003).

You Can't Be Neutral on a Moving Train: A Personal History of Our Times, 2nd ed. (Beacon Press, 2002).

Terrorism and War, with Anthony Arnove (Seven Stories Press/Open Media Series, 2002).

Emma (South End Press, 2002).

Three Strikes: Miners, Musicians, Salesgirls, and the Fighting Spirit of Labor's Last Century, with Dana Frank and Robin D. G. Kelley (Beacon Press, 2001).

Howard Zinn on War (Seven Stories Press, 2001).

Howard Zinn on History (Seven Stories Press, 2001).

La otra historia de los Estados Unidos (Seven Stories Press, 2001).

Marx in Soho: A Play on History (South End Press, 1999).

The Future of History: Interviews with David Barsamian (Common Courage Press, 1999).

The Zinn Reader: Writings on Disobedience and Democracy (Seven Stories Press, 1997).

Failure to Quit: Reflections of an Optimistic Historian (Common Courage Press, 1993; rpt. ed. South End Press, 2002).

The Politics of History, 2nd ed. (University of Illinois, 1990).

Justice: Eyewitness Accounts (Beacon Press, 1977; rpt. ed. South End Press, 2002).

Postwar America: 1945–1971 (Bobbs-Merrill, 1973; rpt. ed. South End Press, 2002).

Disobedience and Democracy: Nine Fallacies of Law and Order (Vintage, 1968; rpt. ed. South End Press, 2002).

Vietnam: The Logic of Withdrawal (Beacon Press, 1967; rpt. ed. South End Press, 2002).

(Ed.) *New Deal Thought* (Bobbs-Merrill, 1966).

SNCC: The New Abolitionists (Beacon Press, 1964; rpt. ed. South End Press, 2002).

The Southern Mystique (Knopf, 1964; rpt. ed. South End Press, 2002).

LaGuardia in Congress (Cornell University, 1959).

The Twentieth Century: A People's History (HarperCollins/Perennial, 2003; 2006).

A People's History of Empire (Metropolitan Books, 2008).

Three Plays: The Political Theater of Howard Zinn (Beacon Press, 2010).

Uncommon Sense (Paradigm Press, 2009).

THE BOMB

Howard Zinn, England, 1945.

THE BOMB

Howard Zinn

Open Media Series | City Lights Books

The Open Media Series is edited by Greg Ruggiero and archived by the Tamiment Library at New York University.

Cover design by Pollen, New York

City Lights Books would like to acknowledge our colleagues at Iwanami Shoten who are releasing a translation of this book in Japan simultaneously with the publication of this edition in the United States. We would also like to thank the diligent team at Translators United for Peace for their thoroughness and attention to detail: Yukari Miyamae, Kazuyo Kishimoto, Katsuki Fukunaga, Hisataka Yamasaki, and translator Masako Arai, who personally went to the library in Royan, France, to research, fact-check, and reference the original documents Howard Zinn studied when he visited the library.

"The Bombing of Royan" is derived from a section of Howard Zinn's *The Politics of History*, published by University of Illinois Press.

Library of Congress Cataloging-in-Publication Data
Zinn, Howard, 1922–2010.
 The bomb / by Howard Zinn.
    p. cm. — (Open media series)
 Includes bibliographical references.
 ISBN 978-0-87286-509-9
1. World War, 1939–1945—Aerial operations, American. 2. Hiroshima-shi (Japan)—History—Bombardment, 1945. 3. Royan (France)—History, Military—History—20th century. I. Title. II. Series.

 D790.Z57 2010
 940.54'2521954—dc22

2010003645

City Lights Books are published at the City Lights Bookstore,
261 Columbus Avenue, San Francisco, CA 94133.
www.citylights.com

Contents

Acts of Rebellion, Large and Small

By Greg Ruggiero

Long before Howard Zinn became a household name, he was revered by activists and educators as one of America's preeminent scholars, historians, and trusted allies of movements for peace and justice. His work was rooted in the disobedient tradition of the abolitionists, suffragists, labor organizers, and anti-war protesters whose struggles have dramatically changed both the legal fabric and the political consciousness of the country. A radical analysis of the structures of power formed the basis of his teaching, writing, and activism. His stature as a public figure and moral compass seemed only to increase with each passing year, until at some point Zinn genuinely *did* become a household name, not as a celebrity but as a vitally important and popularly referenced American intellectual, like Noam Chomsky or Carl Sagan. Perhaps Matt Damon's references to Zinn in the 1997 film *Good Will Hunting* marked the cultural moment when Howard and his masterpiece, *A People's History of the United States*, entered media-driven mass culture. The film certainly helped get the message out about the book. Not long after that *A People's History* sold its millionth copy, and before too long it was no longer a surprise to see Howard and his books in the corporate press and on TV, even in such unlikely programs as *The Simpsons* and *The Sopranos*.[1]

I was first introduced to Howard in 1991 through my friend David Barsamian of Alternative Radio. In January of that year some friends and I had launched the Open Media Series, and a transcript of Zinn's anti-war speech *Power, History, and Warfare* was published a few months later. It was the first of many pamphlets and books by Howard that I have had the privilege to publish.

I learned many things working with Howard, and projects we worked on together were almost always timed to help leverage specific political interventions. For example, his second contribution to the series was *Columbus, the Indians, and Human Progress: 1492–1992*. Published as #19 in May 1992, the pamphlet was created to support indigenous opposition to the fanfare accompanying the 500th-anniversary celebrations of the "discovery" of America. Instead of extolling Christopher Columbus, Howard wanted to raise awareness of Columbus's greed and cruelty by focusing on his true mission—gold—and the countless indigenous people he and his underlings abused and killed in order to get it. The pamphlet ends with the following words:

> In rethinking our history, we are not just looking at the past but at the present, and trying to look at it from the point of view of those who have been left out of the benefits of so-called civilization. It is a simple but profoundly important thing we are trying to accomplish, to look at the world from other points of view. We need to do that, as we come into the next century, if we want this coming century to be different, if we want it to be not an American century, or a Western century, or a white century, or a male century, or any nation's, any group's century, but a century for the human race.

The third Zinn title in the Open Media Series was also written and published as a timed intervention—a concise counternarrative to the fiftieth anniversary of the U.S. atomic attacks on Japan. At the time it was written, reflections on U.S. actions in World War II were widely couched in feel-good terms like "the good war" and "the greatest generation" and delivered via uncritical presentations like the Smithsonian Institution's Air and Space

Museum exhibit, dominated by the fuselage of the *Enola Gay* and archival footage of its smiling crew. In opposition to the atomic bombings of Hiroshima and Nagasaki and to the very premise of a "good war," Howard wrote *Hiroshima: Breaking the Silence*, first published in June 1995 as pamphlet #34 in the Open Media Series and presented again here.

Howard's feelings and views about the U.S. atomic attacks on Japan were always conveyed with a fresh sense of urgency. He spoke out frequently against the immorality of the U.S. bombings of Hiroshima and Nagasaki, against the madness of nuclear weapons, and against the inevitable consequences of such weapons—the indiscriminate killing and injury of ordinary people. Even after it had sold thousands of copies and had long gone out of print, *Hiroshima: Breaking the Silence* remained important to him. After we worked together on his 2006 book with City Lights, *A Power Governments Cannot Suppress*, he and I discussed the upcoming sixty-fifth anniversary of the bombings and made plans for this book. Howard said he would like to bring the Hiroshima text back into print, and suggested combining it with an earlier essay he'd written about the U.S. napalm-bombing of Royan, France—a combat mission in which he participated in April 1945. We decided to call it *The Bomb*, and that Howard would open the book with a new introduction. In December 2009, one month before he passed away in Los Angeles, Howard emailed me the new introduction and the book was complete—another small act of rebellion against official versions of history and justifications for war.

Howard loved small acts of rebellion. He loved them because it's through small acts that all big change begins, and shifting historical focus from the wealthy and powerful to the ordinary person was perhaps his greatest act of rebellion and incitement. For Howard, to refuse to comply with injustice is to participate in the making of the people's history, and to stand up, speak out, argue against official narratives, form oppositional networks, take to the streets and disobey are among our non-negotiable rights, and the more people we connect with while we rebel, the greater the joy.[2]

As I write this during the first week of April 2010, President Obama has released the latest U.S. "Nuclear Posture Review." Along with declaring plans for limited reduction of aging nuclear weapons and making vague reference to their eventual elimination at some unspecified time beyond his term of office, the commander-in-chief's announcement clearly reasserts the U.S. military plan to possess and potentially use nuclear weapons against the populations of other countries. While an op-ed in the *New York Times* responded with the statement, "No one in their right mind can imagine the United States ever using a nuclear weapon again,"[3] that is precisely what the United States is doing by keeping thousands of nuclear weapons ready for attack by land, air and sea.

I think Howard would agree with the anonymous op-ed writer and add that the Obama administration is not in its right mind. Not only does the new nuclear doctrine assert conditions under which the U.S. would use nuclear weapons again, but President Obama used the release of the new policy as an opportunity to intensify threats against North Korea and Iran.

Zinn's argument is urgent and direct: there simply is no situation, however atrocious, to ever justify us to allow the leaders of this country to attack with nuclear weapons again:

> It is a prescription for the endless cycle of violence and counter-violence, terrorism and counter-terrorism, that has plagued our times, for which the only response is: "No more wars or bombings, of retaliation. *Someone*, no, *we*, must stop that cycle, now."
>
> The strategic argument, which I and other historians have tried to answer with the evidence that there was no military necessity to use the bomb, is not enough. We need to confront the moral issue directly: faced with the horrors

visited on hundreds of thousands of human beings by the massive bombings of modern warfare,
can any military-strategic-political "necessity"
justify that?

And if the answer is no, as I believe, what can
we learn to free us from the thinking that leads us
to stand by . . . while atrocities are committed in
our name?

May this little book contribute to our collective asking
of that question, loudly, and to answering it, in Howard's
spirit, with acts of rebellion large and small.

Introduction

By Howard Zinn

The day the war in Europe ended—V-E Day, May 8, 1945—my B-17 bomber crew drove from our airfield in East Anglia to the nearby city of Norwich to join an exultant celebration of victory. The city that had been darkened by blackouts for the past five years of war was now ablaze with lights, and it seemed every man, woman, and child was in the streets, dancing, shouting, weeping with joy, passing around fish and chips and beer and embracing one another.

That July we flew back home—crossing the Atlantic in the same four-engine bomber from which we had dropped bombs on Germany, Czechoslovakia, Hungary, France. We were given a thirty-day furlough to reunite with wives, sweethearts, family, and then we were to head for the Pacific to fly more bombing missions against Japan.

My wife Roslyn and I decided to take a holiday in the country, and as we walked to a bus stop to take us to up-state New York we passed a newsstand and a pile of news-papers with huge black headlines: "Atom Bomb Dropped on Hiroshima." I remember our reaction: *we were happy*. We didn't know what an atom bomb was, but clearly it was huge and important and it foretold an end to the war against Japan, and if so I wouldn't be going to the Pacific, and might soon be coming home for good.

I had no understanding at that moment of what the atomic bomb had done to the people of Hiroshima. It was an abstraction, a headline, just another bombing, like those we had done in Europe, though on a larger scale, it seemed. To this day, the vicious reality of aerial bombing is lost to most people in the United States, a military operation devoid of human feeling, a news event, a statistic, a fact to be taken in quickly and forgotten.

Indeed, that's how it is for those who drop bombs, for people like me, a bombardier sitting in the Plexiglas nose of a B-17, operating my bombsight, observing flashes of light below as the bombs hit, but seeing no human beings, hearing no screams, seeing no blood, totally unaware that down below there might be children dying, rendered blind, with arms or legs severed.

True, I was dropping bombs from 30,000 feet in the air, six miles high, and today's jet bombers are closer to the ground and use the most sophisticated computers to aim their bombs more accurately at their targets. But the operation is just as impersonal, because even in what is called "pinpoint bombing" the man dropping the bomb sees no human beings. He may do what I could never do in World War II, aim at and hit a specific house, a specific automobile. But he has no idea who is in that house, who is in that auto. He has been told by "intelligence"—that monumental misnomer—that the house or the car contains one or more "suspected terrorists."

What you see over and over again in the news reports is the words "suspected terrorist" or "suspected Al Qaeda" —meaning that "intelligence" is not sure whom we are bombing, that we are willing to justify the killing of a "suspect" in Iraq or Afghanistan or Pakistan, something we would not accept from a police operation in New York or San Francisco. This suggests, to our shame, that the lives of people other than Americans are of lesser importance.

In this way, the members of a wedding party in Afghanistan were put to death by an American bombing aimed at "suspected terrorists." Immediately after Obama's election, unmanned "Predator" drone missiles were fired on Pakistan. In the second of these strikes, as Jane Mayer reported in an analysis in the *New Yorker* of Predator bombing, the house of a pro-government tribal leader was wrongly targeted (by "intelligence"). "The blast killed the tribal leader's entire family, including three children, one of them five years old."

In World War II the equipment was not as sophisticated, but the results were the same: innocent people killed. The bombardiers of today are in the same position I was in, following orders without question, oblivious of the human consequences of our bombing.

Not until I was out of uniform did I have an awakening, the shock of understanding. It came from reading John Hersey's account of his interviews in Hiroshima with survivors of the bombing, who told their stories in the most graphic and horrifying detail: "The eyebrows of some were burned off and skin hung from their faces and hands. Others, because of pain, held their arms up as if carrying something in both hands."

John Hersey's dispatches made me think of my own bombing missions, and how I had mindlessly dropped bombs on cities without thinking of what human beings on the ground were experiencing. I particularly thought of my last bombing mission.

It took place three weeks before the end of the war in Europe, and everyone knew the war was essentially over. The bomber crews on our airfield in East Anglia expected that there would be no more missions over Europe. Surely there was no reason to do any more bombing, not even the crass justification of "military necessity."

But we were awakened from our sleeping bags in the corrugated tin huts we lived in and ordered onto trucks to take us to the briefing rooms and the flight line. It was about three in the morning, the usual wake-up time on days we were flying missions, because there would be three hours for intelligence briefings, breakfast, and equipment checking before taking off at dawn.

At the briefing, we were told we were going to bomb a German garrison stationed near the town of Royan, a vacation spot on the Atlantic Coast of France not far from the port of Bordeaux. The Germans weren't attacking, just sitting there waiting for the war to end, and we would wipe them out.

In the summer of 1966 I spent some time in Royan and found in the town library most of the material on which my essay is based.

Hiroshima
Breaking the Silence

The bomb dropped on Hiroshima on August 6, 1945, turned into powder and ash, in a few moments, the flesh and bones of 140,000 men, women, and children. Three days later, a second atomic bomb dropped on Nagasaki killed perhaps 70,000 instantly. In the next five years, another 130,000 inhabitants of those two cities died of radiation poisoning.

No one will ever know the exact figures, but these come from the most exhaustive report available, *Hiroshima and Nagasaki: The Physical, Medical, and Social Effects of the Atomic Bombings*, put together by a team of thirty-four Japanese scientists and physicians, then translated and published in this country in 1981. Those statistics do not include countless other people who were left alive, but maimed, poisoned, disfigured, blinded.

We live in a time where our minds have been so

battered by the statistics of death and suffering that figures in the millions leave us numb, and nothing but the
personal testimonies of individuals—even if they can only
faintly represent the reality—are capable of shaking us out
of that numbness.

A Japanese schoolgirl, 16 years old at the time, re-
called years later that it was a beautiful morning. She saw
a B-29 fly by, then a flash. She put her hands up and "my
hands went right through my face." She saw "a man without feet, walking on his ankles." She passed out. "By the
time I wake up, black rain was falling. . . . I thought I was
blind, but I got my eyes open, and I saw a beautiful blue sky
and the dead city. Nobody is standing up. Nobody is walking around. . . . I wanted to go home to my mother."

This was Kinuko Laskey, speaking in broken English
at a U.S. Senate hearing in Washington, D.C. We need to
recall her testimony and that of others: "A woman with her
jaw missing and her tongue hanging out of her mouth was
wandering around . . . in the heavy black rain . . . crying
for help."

In *The Making of the Atomic Bomb*, probably the most
thorough and vivid narrative of that long, costly, and secret
enterprise on the New Mexico desert known as "The Manhattan Project," Richard Rhodes, scrupulously controlled
up to this point, describes the results with unmistakable
feeling:

People exposed within half a mile of the Little Boy fireball were seared to bundles of smoking black char in a fraction of a second as their internal organs boiled away.... The small black bundles now stuck to the streets and bridges and sidewalks of Hiroshima numbered in the thousands. At the same instant birds ignited in midair. Mosquitoes and flies, squirrels, family pets crackled and were gone.

Robert Jay Lifton, a psychiatrist who refused to work within the orthodox limits of his profession, was one of the first, in his book, *Death In Life*, to interview survivors. A college girl in her junior year at Hiroshima remembered: "The faces of my friends who just before were working energetically are now burned and blistered, their clothes torn to rags. . . . Our teacher is holding her students close to her like a mother hen protecting her chicks, and like baby chicks paralyzed with terror, the students were thrusting their heads under her arms."

A woman, then a girl in the fifth grade, remembered: "Everybody in the shelter was crying out loud. . . . I do not know how many times I called begging that they would cut off my burned arms and legs."

One of the first of American journalists on the scene after the bombing was John Hersey. His articles in the *New*

Yorker were reproduced in the book *Hiroshima* and delivered the first shock to an American public still celebrating the end of the war. Hersey interviewed six survivors: a clerk, a tailor's widow, a priest, a doctor, a surgical assistant, a pastor. He found that of one hundred and fifty doctors in the city, sixty-five were already dead and most of the rest were wounded. Of 1,780 nurses, 1,654 were dead or so badly wounded that they could not work. Hersey reported on his interview of the pastor, "Mr. Tanimoto . . . reached down and took a woman by the hands, but her skin slipped off in huge, glove-like pieces. He was so shocked by this that he had to sit down for a moment. . . . He had to keep consciously repeating to himself, 'These are human beings.'"

Only with those scenes in our minds can we judge the distressingly cold arguments that go on now, sixty-five years later, about whether it was right to send those planes out those two mornings in August of 1945. That this is arguable is a devastating commentary on our moral culture.

And yet, the arguments must be met, because they continue to be advanced, in one form or another, every time the organized power of the state is used to commit an atrocity—whether the setting is Auschwitz or My Lai or Chechnya or Waco, Texas, or Philadelphia, where families in the MOVE organization were firebombed by the police.

When private bands of fanatics commit atrocities we call them "terrorists," which they are, and have no trouble dismissing their reasons. But when governments do the same, and on a much larger scale, the word "terrorism" is not used, and we consider it a sign of our democracy that the acts become subject to debate. If the word "terrorism" has a useful meaning (and I believe it does, because it marks off an act as intolerable, since it involves the indiscriminate use of violence against human beings for some political purpose), then it applies exactly to the bombings of Hiroshima and Nagasaki.

The sociologist Kai Erikson, reviewing the report by the Japanese team of scientists, wrote:

> The attacks on Hiroshima and Nagasaki were not "combat" in any of the ways that word is normally used. Nor were they primarily attempts to destroy military targets, for the two cities had been chosen not despite but because they had a high density of civilian housing. Whether the intended audience was Russian or Japanese or a combination of both, then the attacks were to be a show, a display, a demonstration. The question is: What kind of mood does a fundamentally decent people have to be in, what kind of moral arrangements must it make, before it is willing to annihilate as

many as a quarter of a million human beings for the sake of making a point.

Let's leave aside the phrase "a fundamentally decent people," which raises troubling questions: Are Americans more deserving of that description than others? Are not all atrocities committed by "fundamentally decent people" who have been maneuvered into situations that derange the sense of morality common to all human beings?

Rather, let's examine the question properly raised by Kai Erikson, a question enormously important precisely because it does not permit us to dismiss horrors as acts inevitably committed by horrible people. It forces us to ask: what "kind of mood," what "moral arrangements" would cause us, in whatever society we live, with whatever "fundamental decency" we possess, to either perpetrate (as bombardiers, or atomic scientists, or political leaders), or to just accept (as obedient citizens), the burning of children in vast numbers.

That is a question not just about some past and ir-retrievable event involving someone else, but about all of us, living today in the midst of outrages different in detail but morally equivalent, to Hiroshima and Nagasaki. It is about the continued accumulation by nations (ours being first) of atomic weapons a thousand times more deadly, ten thousand times more numerous, than those first bombs. It is about the expenditure each year of a trillion dollars for these and what are soberly called "conventional" weapons, while fourteen million children die each year for lack of food or medical care.

We would need, then, to examine the psychological and political environment in which the atomic bombs could be dropped and defended as legitimate, as necessary. That is, the climate of World War II.

It was a climate of unquestioned moral righteousness. The enemy was Fascism. The brutalities of Fascism were undisguised by pretense: the concentration camps, the murder of opponents, the tortures by secret police, the burning of books, the total control of information, the roving gangs of thugs in the streets, the designation of "inferior" races deserving extermination, the infallible leader, the mass hysteria, the glorification of war, the invasion of other countries, the bombing of civilians. No literary work of imagination could create a more monstrous evil. There was, indeed, no reason to question that the enemy in World War II was monstrous and had to be stopped before it enveloped more victims.

But it is precisely that situation—where the enemy is undebatably evil—that produces a righteousness dangerous not only to the enemy but to ourselves, to countless innocent bystanders, and to future generations.

We could judge the enemy with some clarity. But not

ourselves. If we did, we might have noted some facts cloud-ing the simple judgment that since they were unquestion-ably evil, we were unquestionably good.

The pronoun "we" is the first deception, because it merges the individual consciences of the citizenry with the motives of the state. If our (the citizens') moral intent in making war is clear—in this case the defeat of Fascism, the halt to international aggression—we assume the same intent on the part of "our" government. Indeed, it is the government that has proclaimed the moral issues in order to better mobilize the population for war, and encouraged us to assume that we, government and citizens, have the same objectives.

There is a long history to that deception, from the Peloponnesian wars of the fifth century before Christ through the Crusades and other "religious" wars, into mod-ern times, when larger sections of population must be mo-bilized, and the technology of modern communication is used to advance more sophisticated slogans of moral purity.

As for our country, we recall expelling Spain from Cuba, ostensibly to liberate the Cubans, actually to open Cuba to our banks, railroads, fruit corporations, and army. We conscripted our young men and sent them into the slaughterhouse of Europe in 1917 to "make the world safe for democracy." (Note how difficult it is to avoid the "we," the "our," that assimilates government and people into an indistinguishable body, but it may be useful to remind us that we're responsible for what the government does.)

In World War II, the assumption of a common motive for government and citizen was easier to accept because of the obvious barbarity of Fascism. But can we accept the idea that England, France, the United States, with their long history of imperial domination in Asia, in Africa, the Middle East, Latin America, were fighting against international aggression? Against German, Italian, Japanese aggression certainly. But against their own?

Indeed, although the desperate need for support in the war brought forth the idealistic language of the Atlantic Charter with its promise of self-determination, when the war ended, the colonized people of Indochina had to fight against the French, the Indonesians against the Dutch, the Malaysians against the British, the Africans against the European powers, and the Filipinos against the United States in order to fulfill that promise.

The question of "motive" for the United States in making war against Japan is put this way by Bruce Russett in his book, *No Clear and Present Danger*:

Throughout the 1930s the United States government had done little to resist the Japanese advance on the Asian continent. [But:] The Southwest Pacific area was of undeniable economic importance to the United States—at the time most of America's tin and rubber came from there, as did substantial quantities of other raw materials.

A year before Pearl Harbor, a State Department memorandum on Japanese expansion did not talk of the independence of China or the principle of self-determination. Again on the American motive, it said:

> . . . our general diplomatic and strategic position would be considerably weakened—by our loss of Chinese, Indian and South Seas markets (and by our loss of much of the Japanese market for our goods, as Japan would become more and more self-sufficient) as well as by insurmountable restrictions upon our access to the rubber, tin, jute, and other vital materials of the Asian and Oceanic regions.

That has a familiar sound. Shortly after World War II, in the early 1950s, massive American aid to the French (who were fighting to hold on to their pre-war colony of Indochina) was accompanied by righteous declarations of the need to fight Communism. But the internal memoranda of National Security Council were talking of the U.S. need for tin, rubber, and oil.

There were pious statements about self-determination, noble words in the Atlantic Charter that the Allies "seek no aggrandizement, territorial or other." However, two weeks before the Charter, U.S. Acting Secretary of State Sumner Welles was assuring the French government: "This Government, mindful of its traditional friendship for France, has deeply sympathized with the desire of the French people to maintain their territories and to preserve them intact."

It is understandable that the pages of the Defense Department's official history of the Vietnam War (The Pentagon Papers) were marked "TOP SECRET—Sensitive," because they revealed that in late 1942 President Roosevelt's personal representative assured French General Henri Giraud: "It is thoroughly understood that French sovereignty will be re-established as soon as possible throughout all the territory, metropolitan or colonial, over which flew the French flag in 1939."

As for the motives of Stalin and the Soviet Union—it is absurd to even ask if they were fighting against the police state, against dictatorship. Yes, against German dictatorship, the Nazi police state, but not their own. Before, during, and after the war against Fascism, the fascism of the gulag persisted, and expanded.

And if the world might be deluded into thinking that the war was fought to end military intervention by great powers in the affairs of weaker countries, the post-war years quickly countered that delusion, as the two important victors—the United States and the Soviet Union—sent their armies, or surrogate armed forces, into countries in Central America and Eastern Europe.

Did the Allied powers go to war to save the Jews from persecution, imprisonment, extermination? In the years before the war, when the Nazis had already begun their brutal attacks on the Jews, the United States, England, and France maintained silence. President Roosevelt and Secretary of State Hull were reluctant to put the United States on record against the anti-Jewish measures in Germany.

Shortly after we were at war, reports began to arrive that Hitler was planning the annihilation of the Jews. Roosevelt's administration failed to act again and again when there were opportunities to save Jews. There is no way of knowing how many Jews could have been saved in various ways that were not pursued. What is clear is that saving Jewish lives was not the highest priority.

Hitler's racism was brutally clear. The racism of the Allies, with their long history of the subjugation of colored people around the world, seemed forgotten, except by the people themselves. Many of them, like India's Gandhi, had difficulty being enthusiastic about a war fought by the white imperial powers they knew so well.

In the United States, despite powerful attempts to

mobilize the African American population for the war, there was distinct resistance. Racial segregation was not just a Southern fact, but a national policy. That is, the Supreme Court of the United States, in 1896, had declared such segregation to be lawful, and that was still the law of the land during World War II. It was not a Confederate army but the armed forces of the United States that segregated black from white all through the war.

A student at a black college told his teacher: "The Army Jim Crows us. The Navy lets us serve only as messmen. The Red Cross refuses our blood. Employers and labor unions shut us out. Lynchings continue. We are disenfranchised, Jim Crowed, spat upon. What more could Hitler do than that?"

When NAACP leader Walter White repeated that statement to an audience of several thousand in the Midwest, expecting they would disapprove, instead: "To my surprise and dismay the audience burst into such applause that it took me some thirty or forty seconds to quiet it."

Large numbers of blacks did go along with Joe Louis's famous statement that "There's lots of things wrong here, but Hitler won't cure them." And many were anxious to show their courage in combat. But the long history of American racism cast a cloud over the idealism of the war against Fascism.

There was another test of the proposition that the war

against the Axis powers was in good part a war against racism. That came in the treatment of Japanese Americans on the West Coast. There was contempt for the Nazis, but with the Japanese there was a special factor, that of race. After Pearl Harbor, Congressman John Rankin of Mississippi said: "I'm for catching every Japanese in America, Alaska, and Hawaii now and putting them in concentration camps. . . . Damn them! Let's get rid of them now!"

Anti-Japanese hysteria grew. Racists, military and civilian, persuaded President Roosevelt that the Japanese on the West Coast constituted a threat to the security of the country, and in February of 1942 he signed Executive Order 9066. This empowered the army, without warrants or indictments or hearings, to arrest every Japanese American on the West Coast, most of them born in the United States—120,000 men, women, and children—to take them from their homes, and transport them to "detention camps," which were really concentration camps.

Michi Weglyn, who was a small girl removed from her home with her family, responded to Roosevelt's description of the bombing of Pearl Harbor as "a date that will live in infamy" by writing a book she titled *Years of Infamy*. In it, she tells of the misery, confusion, anger, and also of resistance, strikes, petitions, mass meetings, riots against camp authorities.

John Dower, in *War Without Mercy*, documents the

racist atmosphere that developed quickly, both in Japan and in the United States. *Time* magazine said: "The ordinary unreasoning Jap is ignorant. Perhaps he is human. Nothing . . . indicates it."

Indeed, the Japanese army had committed terrible atrocities in China, in the Philippines. So did all armies, everywhere, but Americans were not considered subhuman, although as Pacific war correspondent Edgar Jones reported, U.S. forces "shot prisoners, wiped out hospitals, strafed lifeboats."

We did do indiscriminate bombing—not atomic, but with enormous civilian casualties—of German cities. Yet, we know that racism is insidious, intensifying all other factors. And the persistent notion that the Japanese were less than human probably played some role in the willingness to wipe out two cities populated by people of color.

In any case, the American people were prepared, psychologically, to accept and even applaud the bombing of Hiroshima and Nagasaki. One reason was that although some mysterious new science was involved, it seemed like a continuation of the massive bombing of European cities that had already taken place.

No one seemed conscious of the irony—that one of the reasons for general indignation against the Fascist powers was their history of indiscriminate bombing of civilian populations. Italy had bombed civilians in

Ethiopia in its conquest of that country in 1935. Japan had bombed Shanghai, Nanking, other Chinese cities. Germany and Italy had bombed Madrid, Guernica, and other Spanish cities in that country's civil war. At the start of World War II, Nazi planes dropped bombs on the civilian populations of Rotterdam in Holland, and Coventry in England.[1]

Franklin D. Roosevelt described these bombings as "inhuman barbarism that has profoundly shocked the conscience of humanity." But very soon, the United States and Britain were doing the same thing, and on a far larger scale. The Allied leaders met in Casablanca in January 1943 and agreed on massive air attacks to achieve "the destruction and dislocation of the German military, industrial and economic system and the undermining of the morale of the German people to the point where their capacity for armed resistance is fatally weakened."

This euphemism—"undermining of the morale"— was another way of saying that the mass killing of ordinary civilians by carpet-bombing was now an important strategy of the war. Once used in World War II, it would become generally accepted after the war, even as nations were dutifully signing on to the U.N. Charter pledging to end "the scourge of war." It would become American policy in Korea, in Vietnam, Iraq, and Afghanistan.

In short, terrorism, condemned by governments when

conducted by nationalist or religious extremists, was now being adopted as official policy. It was given legitimacy because it was used to defeat certain Fascist powers. But it kept alive the spirit of Fascism.

In November of 1942, the chief of the British Air Staff, Sir Charles Portal, suggested that in 1943 and 1944 1.5 million tons of bombs could be dropped on Germany, destroying six million homes, killing 900,000 people, and seriously injuring a million more. British historian John Terraine, writing about this in his book *The Right of the Line*, calls this "a prescription for massacre, nothing more nor less."

With American agreement, Churchill and his advisers decided on the bombing of working-class districts in German cities, and the saturation bombing began. There were thousand-planes raids on Cologne, Essen, Frankfurt. In the summer of 1943, the bombing of Hamburg created what came to be known as a *feuersturm*, a firestorm, in which intense heat created by the bombs sucked out the air, bringing hurricane-like winds that spread the flames throughout the city.

In February of 1945, British planes flying at night created firestorms in Dresden, and U.S. planes flying in the daytime compounded the burning of the city. It was a city crowded with refugees, and no one knows how many died. At least 35,000. Perhaps 100,000. Kurt Vonnegut gave us some sense of the horror of this in his novel *Slaughterhouse Five*.

In his wartime memoirs Churchill described the event tersely: "We made a heavy raid in the latter month on Dresden, then a center of communication of Germany's Eastern Front." The British pilot of a Lancaster bomber was more explicit: "There was a sea of fire covering in my estimation some 50 square miles."

One incident remembered by survivors is that on the afternoon of February 14, 1945, American fighter planes machine-gunned clusters of refugees on the banks of the Elbe. A German woman told of this years later: "We ran along the Elbe stepping over the bodies."

The actor Richard Burton, who was engaged to play the role of Winston Churchill in a television drama, wrote afterward:

> In the course of preparing myself . . . I realized fresh that I hate Churchill and all of his kind. They have stalked down the corridors of endless power all through history. . . . What man of sanity would say on hearing of the atrocities committed by the Japanese . . . "We shall wipe them out, everyone of them, men, women and children. There shall not be a Japanese left on the face of the earth." Such simple-minded cravings

for revenge leave me with a horrified but reluctant awe for such . . . ferocity.

The British flew at night and did "area bombing," with no pretense of aiming at specific military targets. The Americans flew in the daytime, pretending to precision, but bombing from high altitudes made that impossible. (When I was doing my practice bombing in Deming, New Mexico, before going overseas, our egos were built up by having us fly at 4,000 feet and drop a bomb within twenty feet of the target. But at 11,000 feet, we were more likely to miss by 200 feet. Flying combat missions at 30,000 feet, we might miss by a quarter of a mile.)

There was huge self-deception, not among the political leaders who consciously made the decisions, but on the part of the lower-level military who carried them out. We had been angered when the Germans bombed cities and killed several hundred or a thousand people. But now the British and Americans were killing tens of thousands in a single air strike. Michael Sherry, in his classic study, *The Rise of American Air Power*, notes, "so few in the air force asked questions." (I certainly did not, participating in a napalm bombing of the French town of Royan a few weeks before the end of the war in Europe.)

Journalists and writers, enlisted in the propaganda campaign, went along with government policy. John

Steinbeck, in his book *Bombs Away*, said: "We were all part of the war effort."

One month after the Dresden bombing, on March 10, 1945, three hundred B-29's flew over Tokyo at low altitude, with cylinders of napalm and 500-pound clusters of magnesium incendiaries. It was after midnight. Over one million people had evacuated Tokyo, but six million remained. Fire swept with incredible speed through the flimsy dwellings of the poor. The atmosphere became superheated to 1,800 degrees Fahrenheit. People jumped into the river for protection and were boiled alive. The estimates were of 85,000 to 100,000 dead. They died of oxygen deficiency, carbon monoxide poisoning, radiant heat, direct flames, flying debris, or were trampled to death (Masuo Kato, *The Lost War: A Japanese Reporter's Inside Story*).

Katsumoto Saotome was 12 years old then: "It was like looking at a picture through a red filter, the fire was like a living thing. It ran, just like a creature, chasing us."

That spring there were more such raids on Kobe, Nagoya, Osaka, and in late May another huge bombing of what remained of Tokyo. This was accompanied in the press by continued dehumanization of the enemy. *LIFE* magazine showed a picture of a Japanese person burning to death and commented: "This is the only way."

By the time the decision was made to drop the atomic bomb on Hiroshima, our minds had been prepared. Their side was vicious beyond description. Therefore, whatever we did was morally right. Hitler, Mussolini, Tojo, and their general staffs became indistinguishable from German civilians, or Japanese school children. The U.S. Air Force General Curtis LeMay (the same one who, during the Vietnam war, said: "We will bomb them back to the Stone Age") asserted: "There is no such thing as an innocent civilian."

Franklin D. Roosevelt died in April of 1945. We have no way of knowing if matters would have been different if he had been in the White House instead of Truman when the decision was made. But he was president during the saturation bombings of German and Japanese cities, and there is a tendency to romanticize dead presidents as more beneficent than their successors.

The new president, Harry Truman, was taken aside and told about the Manhattan Project. On May 8, 1945, the war in Europe came to an end. In June, after fighting bloodiest battle of the Pacific War, U.S. forces captured the island of Okinawa, just 500 miles south of Japan. There was nothing now between that and Japan itself.

At this point (I am using the research of Martin Sherwin, *A World Destroyed*, as well as Robert Butow, who interviewed Japanese officials shortly after the war and wrote *Japan's Decision to Surrender*) the Japanese began moving quickly to end the war. After the middle of June, six members of the Japanese Supreme War Council authorized

Foreign Minister Togo to approach the Soviet Union "with a view to terminating the war if possible by September."

Ambassador Sato was sent to Moscow to feel out the possibility of a negotiated surrender. (The Russians, who had promised to come into the war some time after victory in Europe, were still officially at peace with Japan.) And on July 13, Foreign Minister Togo wired Sato: "Unconditional surrender is the only obstacle to peace. . . . It is His Majesty's heart's desire to see the swift termination of the war."

The United States had broken the Japanese code early in the war and thus knew the contents of Togo's telegram. But at the Potsdam Conference later in July (Truman, Churchill, and Stalin meeting for the first time since the end of the European war), the United States and its allies insisted that Japan, already ruined and on the verge of defeat, surrender unconditionally.

Former Ambassador to Japan Joseph Grew and others who knew something about Japanese society had suggested an arrangement just short of unconditional surrender, involving just one condition—allowing Japan to keep its emperor. They argued that this would save countless lives by bringing an early end to the war.

The rejection of this idea suggests that the United States was more anxious to show the world—especially the Soviet Union—its atomic weaponry, than to end the war as soon as possible. Indeed, after the bombs were dropped, and the point made, the United States did accept the postwar sanctity of the emperor.

Were Hiroshima and Nagasaki wiped out to make a point?

We find it hard to comprehend the Holocaust that Germany committed, which perhaps can only be understood as intended to make a point about racial inferiority. Can we then comprehend the killing of 200,000 people to make a point about American power?

Historian-economist Gar Alperowitz's impressive research (*Atomic Diplomacy*) into the papers of the principal figures surrounding President Truman—Secretary of War Henry Stimson, Secretary of the Navy James Forrestal, and Truman's closest personal adviser, James Byrnes—supplies powerful evidence for that conclusion. Henry Stimson told Truman, just before the Potsdam meeting, that the bomb (now tested and ready) was "a royal straight flush and we mustn't be a fool about the way we play it." Byrnes advised the president that the bomb "could let us dictate the terms of ending the war." James Forrestal wrote in his diary that Byrnes was "most anxious to get the Japanese affair over with before the Russians got in."

President Truman's secret diaries were not revealed until 1978. In them Truman referred to one of the messages intercepted by American Intelligence as "the telegram from Jap Emperor asking for peace." And, after Stalin confirmed that the Red Army would march against Japan, Truman wrote: "Fini Japs when that comes about."

It seems he did not want the Japs to be "fini" through Russian intervention but through American bombs. This explains the obvious rush to use the bomb in August, days before the Russians were scheduled to enter the war, and months before any planned invasion of Japan.

The British scientist P M S Blackett, one of Churchill's advisers, wrote (*Fear, War, and the Bomb*) that the dropping of the bomb was "the first major operation of the cold diplomatic war with Russia."

In August of 1994, after a three-year campaign, Gar Alperowitz succeeded in getting 800 pages of intercepted communications released by the National Security Council (which had argued that keeping them secret was vital to "national security"). These, he says, "show that Mr. Truman was personally advised of Japanese peace initiatives through Swiss and Portuguese channels as early as three months before Hiroshima."

Also revealed was the report of a German diplomat to Berlin after talking with a Japanese naval officer on May 5, 1945: "Since the situation is clearly recognized to be hopeless, large sections of the Japanese armed forces would not regard with disfavor an American request for capitulation even if the terms were hard." The official documents showed that U.S. Intelligence analysts passed this up the chain of command.

There has been endless discussion about how many American lives would be lost in an invasion of Japan. Truman said "half a million." Churchill said "a million." These figures were pulled out of the air. Historian Barton Bernstein's research could not find any projection for invasion casualties higher than 46,000.

The whole discussion about casualty figures is pointless. It is based on the premise that there would have to be an American invasion of Japan in order to end the war. But the evidence is clear that the Japanese were on the verge of surrender, that a simple declaration on keeping the position of the Emperor would have brought the war to an end, and no invasion was necessary.

The *New York Times* military analyst Hanson Baldwin wrote, shortly after the war:

> The enemy, in a military sense, was in a hopeless strategic position by the time the Potsdam demand for unconditional surrender was made on July 26. Such then was the situation when we wiped out Hiroshima and Nagasaki. Need we have done it? No one, of course, can be positive, but the answer is almost certainly negative.

The United States Strategic Bombing Survey, whose team interviewed the important Japanese decision-makers right after the war, came to this official conclusion:

> Based on a detailed investigation of all the facts and supported by the testimony of the surviving Japanese leaders involved, it is the Survey's opinion that certainly prior to 31 December, 1945, and in all probability prior to 1 November, 1945, Japan would have surrendered even if the atomic bombs had not been dropped, even if Russia had not entered the war, and even if no invasion had been planned or contemplated.

It does not appear that there was any questioning among Truman and his advisers about whether the bombs should be exploded on Japanese cities. The only problem was to choose the target, and this job was given to the "Interim Committee" headed by Henry Stimson. On James Byrnes's recommendation (Stimson was away) the Interim Committee decided the bomb should be dropped "as soon as possible on a war plant surrounded by workers' homes . . . without prior warning."

Scientists at the University of Chicago, led by Nobel Prize winner James Franck, suggested a demonstration use of the bomb on an unpopulated area to show its power and persuade the Japanese to surrender. At least one member of the Interim Committee agreed—Undersecretary of the Navy Ralph Bard. But the Interim Committee's "Scientific Panel," which included Robert Oppenheimer, the chief scientist in charge of making the bomb, rejected the idea, as did the Committee itself.

Later, Oppenheimer said the Scientific Panel "didn't know beans about the military situation in Japan. . . . But in the back of our minds was the notion that the invasion was inevitable because we had been told that."

General Dwight Eisenhower was a dissenter from the prevailing opinion at the high levels of government. He was briefed by Stimson on the fact that the bomb was about to be used, and later described that meeting:

> During his recitation of the relevant facts, I had been conscious of feelings of depression and so I voiced to him my grave misgivings, first on the basis of my belief that Japan was already defeated and that dropping the bomb was completely unnecessary, and secondly because I thought that our country should avoid shocking world opinion by the use of a weapon whose employment was, I thought, no longer mandatory as a measure to save American lives. . . .

Another dissenter, though it is not clear that he expressed this before bombing, was Admiral William D. Leahy, Chairman of the Joint Chiefs of Staff, who said: "The use of this barbarous weapon at Hiroshima and Nagasaki was of no material assistance in our war against Japan. The Japanese were already defeated and ready to surrender."

The B-29 *Enola Gay*, starting out from the island of Tinian, dropped its bomb on Hiroshima at 8:16 a.m. on August 6, 1945, and it exploded 1,900 feet above the courtyard of Shima Hospital, 550 feet from bombardier Tom Ferebee's aiming point. The pilot, Paul Tibbets, said later: "It was all impersonal."

President Truman's immediate reaction, when told of the bombing, was: "This is the greatest thing in history." (David McCullough's admiring biography of Harry Truman glosses over his involvement with the "greatest thing," that is, one of the greatest barbarities, in history.)

Truman announced: "The world will note that the first bomb was dropped on Hiroshima, a military base." It was an absurd statement. True, there were military contingents in Hiroshima—43,000 military personnel; 250,000 civilians. But the bomb killed everyone in its circle of death, military or not.

It seems that there was no specific decision to drop the bomb on Nagasaki (called "Fat Man"; the Hiroshima bomb was "Little Boy") three days later. The preparations had been made and just went ahead without further thought. According to Peter Wyden (*Day One: Before Hiroshima and After*), "No one ever considered the options of delaying the second bomb drop."

One reason for the absence of discussion may well have been that while the Hiroshima bomb fissioned only uranium atoms, the Nagasaki bomb used plutonium, and there was a question whether the plutonium would work as well. Military operations have often been undertaken not out of military necessity but to try out new weaponry. Human life sacrificed for technological "progress"—that is part of the history of modern "civilization."

The lives sacrificed in war may include not only the "other" but also those on your side who are caught in the crossfire, and this is done without apology, for some larger purpose. On July 31, 1945, Martin Sherwin tells us, a message came from the Air Force headquarters on Guam to some higher body: "Reports prisoner of war sources not verified by photos give location of Allied prisoner-of-war camp, one mile north of center of city of Nagasaki. Does this influence the choice of this target for initial Centerboard operation? Request immediately reply."

The reply came: "Targets previously assigned for Centerboard remain unchanged."

Thus, there were American victims of the American

bombings. In 1977, a scholar working in the Foreign Ministry archives in Japan came across a list of American prisoners who died in the bombing of Hiroshima. The U.S. Army denied knowledge of this and said its personnel files had been destroyed by fire. But a documentary filmmaker named Gary DeWalt found records kept by the Adjutant General that contained many of the names that were on the Foreign Ministry list. The heading was: "Killed In Action, Hiroshima, Japan, August 6, 1945." There were ten prisoners from three air crews a half mile from the aiming point.

Some American prisoners were taken to Hiroshima right after the bombing by a Japanese Christian named Fukui,[2] who later told filmmaker DeWalt: "I ordered the driver to stop, with the funeral pyres still burning in the city, and turned to the American soldiers: "Look there. That blue light is women burning. It is babies burning. Is it wonderful to see the babies burning?"

Several American crewmen who parachuted into Japan after Hiroshima were stabbed, shot, beaten to death by angry civilians—one stoned and clubbed by a crowd on the Aioi Bridge, the aiming point for the Enola Gay.

Those were just a few of the American casualties of American bombing. Over 50,000 airmen died in combat, yet, according to Michael Sherry, there was never any serious investigation of how the massive bombing of cities would lead to victory in the war. A "Committee of Operations Analysts" estimated that firebombing in Japan would kill 560,000 in six cities, but, Sherry says: "As usual, the analysts made no attempt to project how such raids would help to assure final victory. . . ."

Long after the war, in 1992, Father George Zabelka, chaplain to the bomb crews that dropped the bombs on Hiroshima and Nagasaki, was interviewed by the Hartford, Connecticut *Catholic Worker*:

> . . . The destruction of civilians in war was always forbidden by the Church, and if a soldier came to me and asked if he could put a bullet through a child's head, I would have told him absolutely not. . . . But in 1945 Tinian Island was the largest airfield in the world. Three planes a minute would take off from it around the clock. Many of these planes went to Japan with the express purpose of killing not one child or one civilian but of slaughtering hundreds and thousands of children and civilians—and I said nothing. . . . I never preached a single sermon against killing civilians to men who were doing it. Because I was brainwashed. It never entered my mind to publicly protest. . . . I was told it was necessary, told openly by the military and told implicitly by my Church's leadership.

To the best of my knowledge, no American cardinals or bishops were opposing these mass air raids. . . . God was on the side of my country. The Japanese were the enemy.

Father Zabelka returned to Hiroshima and Nagasaki in 1984 as an old man "to meet my God . . . the only kind of God that I could adore and love, a God who lives in human history and suffers with people. I detest and could only fear a god that sat as a depersonalized king above the anguish of humanity." He died shortly after his interview with the *Catholic Worker*.

Like Father Zabelka, no one was asking questions. The scientists who made the bomb, presumably the smartest people around, did not (except for a courageous few) ask questions. Freeman Dyson was a scientist and Operations Analyst with the Royal Air Force Bomber Command. Before the war he had considered himself a Gandhian pacifist. But as the war went on, he kept finding reasons for what was being done, every step of the way. He wrote about this years later in his book *Disturbing the Universe*. Only at the end, the damage done, did he stop and think and conclude: "A good cause can become bad if we fight it with means that are indiscriminately murderous."

The scientists who worked on the bomb, Dyson said, "did not just build the bomb—they enjoyed building it."

Historian Michael Sherry characterized the atmosphere in which the scientists worked as "technological fanaticism."

Was it "technological fanaticism" or just the increasing brutalization of those who had started off with a "good cause" that led the American high command to order, on August 14, 1945, the last day of the war, five days after the obliteration of Nagasaki, a thousand-plane raid on several Japanese cities? The last plane had not yet returned from its mission when Truman announced the end of the war.

Japanese writer Oda Makoto described Osaka, one of the cities bombed on August 14. He was a boy. He went out into the streets when the skies were clear and found, in the midst of the corpses, American leaflets written in Japanese that had been dropped with the bombs: "Your government has surrendered. The war is over."

In his book *Lawrence and Oppenheimer*, Noel Davis describes the scientists in the Manhattan Project as "men who let Oppenheimer take protective custody of their emotions." Oppenheimer was hardly a reliable custodian, for, brilliant scientist as he was, he was as trapped in the fanaticism as all the rest. When he was informed by General Leslie Groves, head of the Manhattan Project, of the Hiroshima bombing, he told Groves (Rhodes, *The Making of the Atomic Bomb*): "Everybody is feeling reasonably good about it, and I extend my heartiest congratulations. It's been a long road." (Did the cautious word "reasonably" represent some twinge of doubt?)

Even for those feeling "reasonably good" there must have been some sobering thoughts when, twelve days after the bombing of Nagasaki, a 24-year-old Los Alamos scientist named Harry Daghlian, doing still another experiment, inadvertently exposed his right hand to a huge dose of radiation. His hands swelled, he became delirious, he felt excruciating internal pain, his hair dropped out, his white corpuscles multiplied, and he died within a month. Did the scientists, did anyone, multiply the image of Harry Daghlian by several hundred thousand and imagine the scenes in Hiroshima and Nagasaki?

Nine days after Daghlian's accident, the Association of Los Alamos Scientists was formed at Los Alamos as a voice of warning against nuclear death in the postwar world.

Some scientists had resisted the general air of triumph. Leo Szilard was in some way responsible for the Manhattan Project, because he had persuaded Albert Einstein to write to Franklin D. Roosevelt back in 1942 urging such an enterprise. Ironically, or perhaps "naturally," Einstein was not allowed in on the secret project. Vannevar Bush, writing to the director of the Institute for Advanced Study in Princeton, where Einstein worked, said: "I wish very much that I could place the whole thing before him . . . but this is utterly impossible in view of the attitude of people here in Washington who have studied into his whole history." (Yes, Einstein had a "history" of pacifism, even of socialism.)

Szilard tried his best to organize some opposition to the dropping of the bomb. Before the bomb had even been tested, Szilard prepared a memorandum for President Roosevelt that anticipated the future: "Perhaps the greatest danger that faces us is the probability that our 'demonstration' of atomic bombs will precipitate a race in the production of these devices between the United States and Russia." (Indeed, twenty-four hours after the Hiroshima bombing, Stalin ordered Soviet scientists to get to work on a bomb.)

When the news came that the bombing had taken place, Szilard wrote a letter to a scientist friend: "I suppose you have seen today's newspapers. Using atomic bombs against Japan is one of the greatest blunders of history."

Calling it a "blunder" did not confront the moral issue directly. But there were those who did.

Dwight Macdonald, who with his wife Nancy produced the wartime magazine *Politics* as an outlet for unorthodox points of view, had expressed himself against the Nazi Holocaust: "What has previously been done only by individual psychopathic killers has now been done by the rulers and servants of a great modern State." After the bombing of Hiroshima, Macdonald wrote:

The CONCEPTS "WAR" AND "PROGRESS" ARE NOW OBSOLETE. . . . THE FUTILITY OF MODERN WARFARE SHOULD NOW BE CLEAR. Must we not now conclude, with Simone Weil, that the technical aspect of war today is the evil, regardless of political factors? Can one imagine that the atomic bomb could ever be used "in a good cause"?

After the firebombing of Tokyo, Macdonald wrote: "I saw no expression of horror or indignation in any American newspaper or magazine of sizeable circulation. We have grown callous to massacre." He referred to the apologists for the bombing at *The Nation* and *The New Republic* as "totalitarian liberals."

Macdonald saw the atomic bomb as "the natural product of the kind of society we have created. . . . Those who wield such destructive power are outcasts from humanity. . . . We must 'get' the modern national state before it 'gets' us."

The British Minister of Information, Brendan Bracken, had said: "Our plans are to bomb, burn, and ruthlessly destroy in every way available the people responsible for creating this war." Dwight Macdonald replied: "How many of the 1,200,000 German civilians your air forces have to date bombed, burned, and ruthlessly destroyed would you say are 'responsible for creating this war'?"

Indeed, much of the argument defending the atomic bombings has been based on a mood of retaliation, as if the children of Hiroshima had bombed Pearl Harbor, as if the civilian refugees crowding into Dresden had been in charge of the gas chambers. Did American children deserve to die because of the massacre of Vietnamese children at My Lai?

If silence and passivity in the presence of evil committed by political leaders is deserving of a death sentence, then the populations of all the great powers do not deserve to live. But only in those ordinary people, rethinking their role, is there a possibility for redemption and change.

Surely, we should understand the Japanese people, caught up in an atmosphere of wartime fanaticism as atrocities were carried out by their government, because that happened in our country. And we should understand the frustration of people who resisted that fanaticism, yet felt powerless to stop what was going on.

Against the claims of a violent "human nature" there is enormous historical evidence that people, when free of a manufactured nationalist or religious hysteria, are more inclined to be compassionate than cruel. When citizens have an opportunity to learn of vicious acts committed by their own governments (as Americans learned during the

Vietnam war, as Russians have learned about their attacks on Chechnya) they react with indignation and protest.

So long as atrocities remain remote, abstract, they will be tolerated, even by decent people. As an Air Force bombardier, returning from the end of the war in Europe, preparing to go on to Japan, I read the headline "Atomic Bomb Dropped on Japan" and was glad; the war would be over. Like other Americans, I had no idea what was going on at the higher levels. And I had no idea what that "atomic bomb" had done to men, women, children in Hiroshima, any more than I ever really understood what the bombs I dropped on European cities were doing to human flesh and blood.

Then I read John Hersey's book *Hiroshima*. And in 1966, my wife and I, in Hiroshima, were invited to a "house of rest" where survivors of the bombing would gather. I was asked, as an American attending a conference to eliminate nuclear weapons, to say a few words. I rose, looked out at my listeners, blind, missing limbs, horribly burned, and my words caught in my throat. I could not speak.

It is a kind of tribute to the moral sensibility of the American people that there have been efforts to prevent the public from getting some sense of what fellow human beings endured in Hiroshima and Nagasaki. (Anyone who wasn't there can hardly know.) It explains why films taken by an Air Force newsreel officer, Lieutenant Daniel

McGovern, in Nagasaki a month after the bombing, and other films collected by him from Japanese photographers, were kept secret for many years.

It explains why, after the Japanese surrender, U.S. military authorities established a Civil Censorship Code, prohibiting all reporting on atomic suffering, making it a crime to write or broadcast data on this. (I get this from an article by Sadao Kamata and Stephen Salaff in the *Bulletin of Concerned Asian Scholars*, 1982.) Only with the peace treaty of 1952 did this code end.

The Smithsonian Institution carried this censorship into our own country when it rejected the offer of the Hiroshima Peace Museum to lend to its exhibit what it held under a glass case—the burned and twisted lunchbox, its contents melted, of a Japanese student named Shigeru Orimen who died instantly under the bomb. A Japanese survivor of the bombing, a 73-year-old woman named Chiyoko Kuwabara, said the Smithsonian decision showed "the arrogance of the victor." She said: "Japan started the war, but that doesn't justify the horror of nuclear weapons."

Down to the present day, the massive bombing of civilians is justified, by intellectuals putting into respectable words the crude and brutish argument: "Sure we committed mass murder. But they started it. Our conscience is clear."

Thus, Alan Cowell, writing in the *New York Times* (February 11, 1995) about the destruction of Dresden:

These people argue that because the target of the British bombing was a civilian residential area, and because the Germans were in retreat, there was little strategic reason for the raids. But the accusations seem more than offset by the sense, particularly so soon after last month's commemoration of the liberation of the Auschwitz Nazi death camp in Poland, that the ultimate blame is . . . with Hitler.

That argument aims the slogan "Never Again" only at them, never at ourselves. It is a prescription for the endless cycle of violence and counterviolence, terrorism and counterterrorism, that has plagued our times, for which the only response is: "No more wars or bombings, of retaliation. *Someone*, no, *we*, must stop that cycle, now."

The strategic argument, which I and other historians have tried to answer with the evidence that there was no military necessity to use the bomb, is not enough. We need to confront the moral issue directly: faced with the horrors visited on hundreds of thousands of human beings by the massive bombings of modern warfare, can any military-strategic-political "necessity" justify that?

And if the answer is no, as I believe, what can we learn to free us from the thinking that leads us to stand by (yes, as the German people stood by, as the Japanese stood by) while atrocities are committed in our name?

We can keep in mind the words of Richard Rhodes, who has studied the history of the atomic bomb probably more closely than anyone:

> The national security state that the United States has evolved toward since 1945 is significantly a denial of the American democratic vision: suspicious of diversity, secret, martial, exclusive, monolithic, paranoid. . . . Other nations have moderated their belligerence and tempered their ambitions without losing their souls. Sweden was once the scourge of Europe. It gave way. . . . Now it abides honorably and peacefully among the nations.

We can be wary of "technological fanaticism," which blinded many of the scientists of the Manhattan Project even more than the flash they saw in the desert, and which still intoxicates our whole culture.

We can reject the belief that the lives of others are worth less than the lives of Americans, that a Japanese child, or an Iraqi child, or an Afghani child is worth less than an American child. We can refuse to accept the idea, which is the universal justification for war, that the means of massive violence are acceptable for "good ends," because we should know by now, even though we are slow learners, that the ugliness of the means is always certain, the goodness of the end always uncertain.

The Bombing of Royan

In mid-April of 1945, a combined air-ground attack completed the destruction of the French seaside resort of Royan, a town of ancient châteaux and lovely beaches (a favorite spot of Picasso) on the Atlantic coast near Bordeaux. It was ten months after D-day, the invasion of Western Europe by Allied Forces—and three weeks before the final surrender of Germany. The official history of the U.S. Army Air Forces in World War II refers briefly to the attack on Royan:

On the 14 through 16 April more than 1,200 American heavies went out each day to drop incendiaries, napalm bombs, and 2,000-pound demolition bombs on stubborn German garrisons still holding out around Bordeaux. The bombing was effective, and French forces soon occupied the region.

According to the official history those bombs were dropped "on stubborn German garrisons." This is misleading. The bombs were dropped in the general vicinity of Royan, where there were German garrisons (mostly outside the town) and where there were also civilian occupants of the town. It was my participation in this mission, as a bombardier with the 490th Bomb Group, that prompted me, after the war, to inquire into the bombing of Royan. At the time, it seemed just another bombing mission, with a slightly different target, and a slightly different cargo of bombs. We were awakened in the early hours of morning, went to the briefing where we were told our job was to bomb pockets of German troops remaining in and around Royan, and that in our bomb bays were thirty 100-pound bombs containing "jellied gasoline," a new substance (now known as napalm). Our bombs were not precisely directed at German installations but were dropped by toggle switch over the Royan area, on seeing the bombs of the lead ship leave the bomb bay—a device good for saturation bombing, not pinpoint bombing (aside from the fact that the Norden bombsight, which we were trained to use, could not be counted on to hit enemy installations and miss nearby civilians from a height of 25,000 feet). The toggle switch was connected to an intervalometer which automatically dropped the bombs, after the first fell, in a timed sequence. From our great height, I remember distinctly seeing the bombs explode in the town, flaring like matches struck in fog. I was completely unaware of the human chaos below.

•   •   •

A letter from Colonel H. A. Schmidt, of the Office of the Chief of Military History, Department of the Army, responding to my request for information on the bombing of Royan, stated:

> The liberation of the port of Bordeaux required the reduction of the bridgeheads of Royan, la Pointe de Grave and Oléron. The Royan sector was the principal German garrison holding out in the Bordeaux area, and first priority in the operations. The Eighth U.S. Air Force paved the way of the Allied ground forces by massive bombing.

The quick, casual description of potentially embarrassing episodes is common in histories written by men in government. Winston Churchill, who was Prime Minister when the city of Dresden was indiscriminately saturated with firebombs in February 1945, leaving 135,000 dead, and who had approved the general strategy of bombing urban areas, confined himself to this comment in his memoirs: "We made a heavy raid in the latter month on Dresden, then a centre of communications of Germany's Eastern front."[1]

Strenuous arguments were made for the bombing attacks on Hiroshima and Dresden on the basis of military necessity, although ultimately the evidence was overwhelmingly against such arguments. In the case of Royan, it was virtually impossible to even launch a defense of the attack on the grounds of military need. It was a small town on the Atlantic coast, far from the fighting front. True, it commanded the sea entrance to Bordeaux, a great port. But this was not crucially needed. Without Bordeaux, and later without its port facilities, the Allies had invaded Normandy, taken Paris, crossed the Rhine, and were now well into Germany. Furthermore, the general air-ground assault on Royan took place three weeks before the end of the war in Europe, at a time when everyone knew it would all soon be over and all one had to do was wait for the German garrisons in the area to surrender.[2]

Nevertheless, on April 14, 1945, the attack on Royan began, and the next day it was reported from London to the *New York Times* as follows:

The full weight of the United States Eighth Air Force was hurled yesterday against one of Europe's forgotten fronts, the German-held pocket in the Gironde Estuary commanding the great southwestern French port of Bordeaux. The blow by 1,150 Flying Fortresses and Liberators, without fighter escort, preceded a limited land attack by French troops. . . .

Some 30,000 to 40,000 Nazi troops have been holed up in the Gironde Estuary pocket since the tides of war swept around and past them last summer. . . . The striking force was probably the biggest heavy bombing fleet ever sent out from Britain in daylight without escorting fighters. Five of the big planes failed to return.

Was the air raid worth even the loss of only five air crews—forty-five men? That was just the tip of the tragedy, counted in lives lost, homes destroyed, persons wounded and burned. For the next day, April 15, the attack was heavier, and the airplanes had a new weapon. A front-page dispatch in the *New York Times* from Paris reported "two days of shattering aerial bombardment and savage ground attacks in the drive to open the port of Bordeaux." It went on:

More than 1,300 Flying Fortresses and Liberators of the United States Eighth Air Force prepared the way for today's successful assault by drenching the enemy's positions on both sides of the Gironde controlling the route to Bordeaux with about 460,000 gallons of liquid fire that bathed in flames the German positions and strong points. . . .

It was the first time that the Eighth Air Force had employed its new bomb. The inflammable substance is dropped in tanks that are exploded on impact by detonators that ignite the fuel, splashing the flaming contents of each tank over an area of approximately sixty square yards.

The liquid fire was napalm, used for the first time in warfare. The following day there was another bombing with high-explosive bombs and further ground assaults. Altogether, it took three days of bombing and land attacks to bring the Germans in the area to surrender. The French ground forces suffered about two hundred dead; the Germans lost several hundred. There is no accurate count on the civilian dead resulting from those attacks, but the *New York Times* dispatch by a correspondent in the area reported:

French troops mopped up most of Royan, on the north side of the river's mouth. . . . Royan, a town of 20,000, once was a vacation spot. About 350 civilians, dazed or bruised by two terrific air bombings in forty-eight hours, crawled from the ruins and said the air attacks had been "such hell as we never believed possible."

Within a few weeks the war in Europe was over. The town of Royan, "liberated," was totally in ruins.

That eve-of-victory attack in mid-April 1945 was the second disaster suffered by Royan at the hands of the Allied Forces. On January 5, 1945, in the darkness before dawn, two waves of heavy British bombers, about an hour apart, flew over Royan, which was still inhabited by about two thousand persons despite a voluntary evacuation in the preceding months. There was no warning, and there were no shelters. The bombs were dropped in the heart of the city (completely missing the German troops, who were outside) within a rectangle marked out by flares dropped by one of the planes. Over a thousand people were killed (some of the estimates are twelve hundred, other fourteen hundred). Several hundred people were wounded. Almost every building in Royan was demolished. The later attack in April came, therefore, on the ruins of buildings and the remnants of families, and made the annihilation of the city complete.

That January bombing has never been adequately explained. One phrase recurs in all the accounts—"*une tragique erreur*." The explanation given by military officials at the time was that the planes were originally scheduled to bomb in Germany, but because of bad weather there, were rerouted to Royan without a map of the German positions. French planes from nearby Cognac were supposed to mark the positions with flares, but this was either not done, or done badly, or the flares were carried away by the wind.[3]

A dispatch written by a local person soon after that bombing, titled "La Nuit Tragique," contained this description:[4]

> Under the German occupation. It is night, calm reigns over the sleeping town, midnight sounds in the Royan church. Then one o'clock, then two. . . . The Royannais sleep, muffled against the chill. Three, four o'clock. A low drone is heard in the distance. Rockets light up the beach. The inhabitants are not afraid; they are tranquil, because they know that Allied airplanes, if these are such, will aim at the German fortifications, and besides, is this not the evening when German supply planes come in? The bell sounds five in the clock tower. Then follows the catastrophe,

brutal, horrible, implacable. A deluge of steel and fire descend on Royan; a wave of 350 planes lets go 800 tons of bombs on the town. Some seconds later, survivors are running around busily aiding the wounded. Cries, death rattles. . . . A woman appeals for help, her head appears alone, her body crushed under an enormous beam.

. . . A whole family is imprisoned in a cave, the water mounts. The rescuers lift their heads— this humming, yet, it is another wave of planes. This achieves the complete destruction of Royan and its inhabitants. Royan has gone down with the civilized world, by the error, the bestiality, the folly of man. [*Royan a sombré en même temps que le monde civilisé, par l'erreur, la bêtise et la folie des hommes.*]

Eight days after the attack, an article appeared in *La Libération* appealing for help: "American friends, you whose Florida beaches have never known such hours, take charge of the reconstruction of Royan!"

In 1948, General de Larminat, who was in charge of French forces in the West (that is, the Bordeaux region) for the last six months of the war, broke a long silence to reply to bitter criticism of both the January and April bombings by local leaders. He exonerated the French military command at Cognac, saying they were not responsible for directing the English planes to Royan. It was, rather, a "tragic error" by the Allied Command; the whole episode was one of the unfortunate consequences of war:[4]

> Will we draw from this an excuse to attack our Allies, who gave countless lives to liberate our country? That would be profoundly unjust. All wars carry these painful errors. Where is the infantryman of 1914–18, and of this war, who has not received friendly shells, badly aimed? How many French towns, how many combat units, have suffered bombing by mistake at the hands of the allied planes? This is the painful ransom, the inevitable ransom of war, against which it is vain to protest, about which it is vain to quarrel. We pay homage to those who died in the war, we help the survivors and repair the ruins; but we do not linger on the causes of these unfortunate events, because in truth there is only a single cause: War, and the only ones truly responsible are those who wanted war.

(Compare this with the explanation of the Dresden bombing given by Air Marshal Sir Robert Saundby:

It was one of those terrible things that sometimes happen in wartime, brought about by an unfortunate combination of circumstances. Those who approved it were neither wicked nor cruel, though it may well be that they were too remote from the harsh realities of war to understand fully the appalling destructive power of air bombardment in the spring of 1945. . . .

It is not so much this or the other means of making war that is immoral or inhumane. What is immoral is war itself. Once full-scale war has broken out it can never be humanized or civilized, and if one side attempted to do so it would be most likely to be defeated. So long as we resort to war to settle differences between nations, so long will we have to endure the horrors, the barbarities and excesses that war brings with it. That, to me, is the lesson of Dresden.)

Some important evidence of the January bombing appeared in 1966 with the publication of the memoirs of Admiral Hubert Meyer, French commander in the Rochefort–La Rochelle area (the two Atlantic ports just north of Royan). Meyer, in September and October 1944, when the Germans, having fled west from the Allied invasion in northern France, were consolidating their pockets on the

Atlantic coast, had begun negotiation with the German commander of La Rochelle–Rochefort, Admiral Schirlitz. In effect, they agreed that the Germans would not blow up the port installations, and in return the French would not attack the Germans. Then the Germans evacuated Rochefort, moving north into the La Rochelle area, to lines both sides agreed on.

In late December 1944, Meyer was asked to travel south along the coast from Rochefort to Royan, where the second German coastal pocket was under the command of Admiral Michahelles, to negotiate a prisoner exchange. In the course of these talks, he was told that the German admiral was disposed to sign an agreement to hold the military *status quo* around Royan, as had been done by Shirlitz at Rochefort–La Rochelle. Meyer pointed out that Royan was different, that the Allies might have to attack the Germans there because Royan commanded Bordeaux, where free passages of goods was needed to supply the Southwest. The Germans, to Meyer's surprise, replied that they might agree to open Bordeaux to all but military supplies.

Conveying this offer to the French military headquarters at Saintes and Cognac, Meyer received a cool response. The French generals could not give a sound military reason for insisting on an attack, but pointed to "*l'aspect moral.*" It would be hard, said General d'Anselme, "to frustrate an ardent desire for battle—a battle where victory was certain—by the army of the Southwest, which had been champing at the bit for months."[6]

Meyer said that with the war virtually won, the morale of the troops was not worth the sacrifice of a town and hundreds of lives for a limited objective, that they did not have the right to kill a single man when the adversary had offered a truce.[7]

Further discussion, he was told, would have to await the return of General de Larminat, who was away.

Meyer left that meeting with the distinct impression that the die was cast for the attack ("*l'impression très nette que les jeux étaient faits, que Royan serait attaquée*"). This was January 2. Three days later, sleeping at Rochefort, he was awakened by the sound of airplanes flying south toward Royan. Those were the British Lancasters, three hundred and fifty of them, each carrying seven tons of bombs.

Meyer adds another piece of information: approximately one month before the January 5 bombing, an American General, Commander of the Ninth Tactical Air Force, came to Cognac to offer the Southwest forces powerful bombing support, and suggested softening the Atlantic pockets by massive aerial bombardments. He proposed that since the Germans did not have aerial defenses for Royan, here were good targets for bomber-crew trainees in England. The French agreed, but insisted the targets be at two points which formed clear enclaves on the ocean, easily distinguishable from the city itself. No more was heard from the Americans, however, until the bombing itself.[8]

As it turned out, not trainees, but experienced pilots did the bombing, and Meyer concludes that even the American general (sent back to the U.S. after this, as a scapegoat, Meyer suggests) was not completely responsible.

Some blame devolved, he says, on the British Bomber Command, and some on the French generals, for not insisting on a point DeGaulle had made when he visited the area in September—that aerial attacks should only be undertaken here in coordination with ground assaults. Meyer concludes, however, that the real responsibility did not rest with the local military commanders. "To wipe out such a city is beyond military decision. It is a serious political act. It is impossible that the Supreme Command [he refers to Eisenhower and his staff] had not been at least consulted." In the event, he says, that the Allies are shocked by his accusations, they should open their military dossiers and, for the first time, reveal the truth.

If by January 1945 (despite von Rundstedt's Christmas counteroffensive in the Ardennes), it seemed clear that the Allies, well into France, and the Russians, having the Germans on the run, were on the way toward victory—then by April 1945 there was little doubt that the war was near its end. The Berlin radio announced on April 15 that the Russians and Americans were about to join forces around the Elbe, and that two zones were being set up for a Germany cut in two. Nevertheless, a major land-air operation was launched April 14 against the Royan pocket, with more than a thousand planes dropping bombs on a German force of 5,500 men, in a town containing at the time probably less than a thousand people.[9]

An article written in the summer of 1946 by a local writer commented on the mid-April assault:

These last acts left a great bitterness in the hearts of the Royannais, because the Armistice followed soon after, an Armistice foreseen by all. For the Royannais, this liberation by force was useless since Royan would have been, like La Rochelle, liberated normally some days later, without new damage, without new deaths, without new ruins. Only those who have visited Royan can give an account of the disaster. No report, no picture or drawing can convey it.

Another local person wrote:[10]

Surely the destruction of Royan, on January 5, 1945, was an error and a crime: but what put the finishing touches on this folly was the final air raid on the ruins, on the buildings partially damaged, and on others remarkably spared on the periphery, with that infernal cargo of incendiary bombs. Thus was accomplished a deadly work of obvious uselessness, and thus was revealed to the world the powerful destructiveness of napalm.

The evidence seems overwhelming that factors of pride, military ambition, glory, and honor were powerful motives in producing an unnecessary military operation. One of the local commanders wrote later: "It would have been more logical to wait for the surrender of Germany and thus to avoid new human and material losses," but one could not "ignore important factors of morale" ("*faire abstraction de facteurs essentiels d'ordre moral*").[11]

In 1947, a delegation of five leaders of Royan met with General de Larminat. After the war, the citizens of Royan had barred de Larminat from the town, in anger at the military operations under his command that had destroyed it, and at the widespread looting of the Royan homes by French soldiers after "liberation." He hoped now to persuade the Royannais that they had made a mistake. The meeting is described by Dr. Pierre Veyssière, former leader of the Resistance in Royan and a holder of the Croix de Guerre, who says he hoped to get an explanation of the "useless sacrifice" of the population of the town, but "my self-deception was total, absolute." He quotes de Larminat saying the French military did not want the enemy "to surrender of his own accord; that would give the impression the Germans were unconquered."[12]

Another member of the French delegation, Dr. Domecq, a former mayor and Resistance leader, responded to General de Larminat also:

> Royan was destroyed by mistake, you say, my general. . . . Those responsible have been punished, the order to attack, a few days before liberation, could not be questioned by the military. . . . The Germans had to feel our power! Permit me, my general, to tell you, once and for all, in the name of those who paid the cost: "La Victoire de Royan" does not exist, except for you.

General de Larminat responded to the criticism in a letter addressed to Paul Métadier.[13] Pride and military ambition, he pointed out, were not sufficient explanations for such a huge operation; one had to seek a larger source: "This pride, this ambition, did not have the power to manufacture the shells which were used, to create the units which were sent, to divert the important aerial and naval forces that participated." De Larminat said that he had prepared the necessary plans for liquidating "*les poches d'Atlantique*" but that he did not judge the date. The date was fixed for him, and he executed the plans.

He ended his reply with an appeal to patriotism: "Must we therefore, throw opprobrium on old combatants because some isolated ones committed acts, unhappily inevitable in wartime? This is how it has been in all the wars of all time. No one ever, that I know, used this as a pretext to reduce the glory and the valour of the sacrifices made by the combatants." He spoke of the "simple, righteous people" who will put "national glory and independence" before "material losses" and "never forget the respect due to those who fought, many of whom sacrificed their lives to a patriotic ideal that the malcontents [*les attentistes*] have always ignored."

Admiral Meyer, who is more sympathetic to de Larminat than most of the general's critics, had watched the attack on Royan from the heights of Médis, and described the scene:

> The weather was clear, the warmth oppressive. Under a fantastic concentration of fire, the enemy positions, the woods, and the ruins of Royan flamed. The countryside and the sky were thick with powder and yellow smoke. One could with difficulty distinguish the mutilated silhouette of the clock tower of Saint-Pierre, which burned like

a torch. I knew that the allied planes were using
for the first time a new kind of incendiary explo-
sive, a kind of jellied gasoline, known as napalm.

De Larminat, he said, had good days and bad days.
And this was one of his bad days, for in the evening after
Royan was taken, and Meyer went to see the General:
"He was visibly satisfied having achieved this brilliant revenge. . . . Without saying that he was intoxicated with
success, the General seemed to me however to have his
appetite stimulated. . . ."

That exultation was felt at all levels. A press correspondent on the scene described the very heavy artillery
bombardment which prepared the attack on the Royan
area: 27,000 shells. Then the first aerial bombing on Sat-
urday, April 14, with high explosives. Then the bombing
all Sunday morning with napalm. By seven that evening
they were in Royan. It was a blazing furnace. ("*La ville est
un brasier.*") The next morning, they could still hear the
clatter of machine guns in the woods nearby. Royan was
still burning. ("*Royan brûle encore.*") The dispatch ends: "It
is a beautiful spring."

With Royan taken, they decided to attack the island of
Oléron, opposite Rochefort. As Meyer says:

The new victory had inflamed the passions of our

soldiers, giving them the idea that nothing could resist them. News from the German front forecast a quick end to the war. Each one wanted a last moment to distinguish himself and get a bit of glory; moderation was scorned, prudence was seen as cowardice.

Meyer did not believe the attack on Oléron was necessary. But he participated assiduously in planning and executing it, happy to be once again involved in a naval operation, and convinced that his duty was only to carry out orders from above.

The attack on Oléron was disputable from the point of view of general strategy. It was a costly luxury, a conquest without military value, on the eve of the war's end. But this was not for me to judge. My duty was limited to doing my best in making those military decisions which would fulfill my orders.

Meyer blames the political leaders above. Yet *blame* seems the wrong word, because Meyer believes it honorable to follow orders, whatever they are, against whatever adversary is chosen for him: "*Quant au soldat, depuis des millénaires, ce n'est plus lui qui forge ses armes et qui choisit son adversaire. Il n'a que le devoir d'obéir dans la pleine mesure de sa foi, de son courage, de sa résistance.*"[14]

One can see in the destruction of Royan that infinite chain of causes, that infinite dispersion of responsibility, that can give infinite work to historical scholarship and sociological speculation, and bring an infinitely pleasurable paralysis of the will. What a complex of motives! In the Supreme Allied Command, the simple momentum of the war, the pull of prior commitments and preparations, the need to fill out the circle, to pile up the victories as high as possible. At the local military level, the ambitions, petty and large, the tug of glory, the ardent need to participate in a grand communal effort by soldiers of all ranks. On the part of the American Air Force, the urge to try out a newly developed weapon. (Paul Métadier wrote: "In effect, the operation was above all characterized by the dropping of new incendiary bombs which the Air Force had just been supplied with. According to the famous formulation of one general: 'They were marvelous!'") And among all participants, high and low, French and Americans, the most powerful motive of all: the habit of obedience, the universal teaching of all cultures, not to get out of line, not even to think about that which one has not been assigned to think about, the negative motive of not having either a reason or a will to intercede.

Everyone can point, rightly, to someone else as being

responsible. In that remarkable film *King and Country*, a simple-minded British country boy in the trenches of World War I walks away one day from the slaughter. He is condemned to death in a two-step process, and although no one thinks he really should be executed, the officers in each step can blame those in the other. The original court sentences him to death thinking to make a strong point and then have the appeals tribunal overturn the verdict. The appeals board, upholding the verdict, can argue that the execution was not its decision. The man is shot. That procedure, one recalls, goes back to the Inquisition, when the church only conducted the trial, and the state carried out the execution, thus confusing both God and the people about the source of the decision.

More and more in our time, the mass production of massive evil requires an enormously complicated division of labor. No one is positively responsible for the horror that ensues. But every one is negatively responsible, because anyone can throw a wrench into the machinery. Not quite, of course—because only a few people have wrenches. The rest have only their hands and feet. That is, the power to interfere with the terrible progression is distributed unevenly, and therefore the sacrifice required varies, according to one's means. In that odd perversion of the natural that we call society (that is, nature seems to equip each species for its special needs) the greater one's capability for interference, the less urgent is the need to interfere.

It is the immediate victims—or tomorrow's—who have the greatest need, and the fewest wrenches. They must use their bodies (which may explain why rebellion is a rare phenomenon). This may suggest to those of us who have a bit more than our bare hands, and at least a small interest in stopping the machine, that we might play a peculiar role in breaking the social stalemate.

This may require resisting a false crusade—or refusing one or another expedition in a true one. But always, it means refusing to be transfixed by the actions of other people, the truths of other times. It means acting on what we feel and think, here, now, for human flesh and sense, against the abstractions of duty and obedience.

Endnotes

Acts of Rebellion, Large and Small

1. Episode 1911 of *The Simpsons*, "That 90s Show," features a younger Marge Simpson with a copy of Zinn's *A People's History of the United States*. Episode three, season four of *The Sopranos* titled "Christopher" centers around Columbus Day and features a reference to Zinn and *A People's History of the United States*.

2. These lines are excerpted from "Teacher, Friend, and Compañero—Howard Zinn," reflections on Howard I wrote in the days following his death in January 2010 and published by *Znet*. Link: www.zcommunications.org/teacher-friend-and-companero-howard-zinn-by-greg-ruggiero.

3. "Mr. Obama's Nuclear Policy," op-ed, April 6, 2010, www.nytimes.com/2010/04/07/opinion/07wed1.html?hpw.

Hiroshima

1. In Rotterdam, 980 were killed in the German raid of May 14, 1940. In Coventry, 380 were killed. See David Irving, *The Destruction of Dresden*, Holt, Reinhart & Winston, 1964, Chapter 1.

2. T. C. Cartwright: A Date with the Lonesome Lady—A Hiroshima POW Returns.

The Bombing of Royan

1. David Irving, *The Destruction of Dresden*, Part II, esp. Ch. II, "Thunderclap," which shows the part Churchill played in pushing the massive raids on cities in Eastern Germany; and Part V, Ch. II, where Churchill later seems to be trying to put the blame on the Bomber Command.

2. Also, in a remark I must confine to a footnote as a gesture to the equality of all victims: there was something to distinguish Royan from both Hiroshima and Dresden; its population was, at least officially, friend, not foe.

3. This is repeated as late as 1965 in Dr. J.R. Colle's book, *Royan, son passé, ses environs* (La Rochelle, 1965), who summarizes, the incident in his chapter, "La Résistance et La Libération."

4. The periodical in which the article appeared is no longer available, but the article, along with many others to which I will refer, was collected in a remarkable little book, produced by a printer in Royan, a former member of the Resistance (Botton, Père et fils) in 1965, titled: *Royan—Ville Martyre*. The translations are mine. A bitter introductory note by Ulysse Botton speaks of "*la tuerie*" (the slaughter) of January 5, 1945. There is a picture of the rebuilt Royan, modern buildings instead of ancient châteaux. "Our visitors, French and foreign vacationers, should thus learn, if they do not know it, that this new town and this modern architecture proceed from a murder, to this day neither admitted nor penalized"

5. Botton collection. This is of course, a widely held view: "c'est la guerre"—a resigned, unhappy surrender to inevitability. We find it again and again in *Le Pays d'Ouest*, a postwar periodical, now defunct, which published an article, "Le Siège et Attaque de Royan," saying: "Whatever the reason, the bombardment of Royan on January 5, 1945, must be considered among the regrettable errors that unfortunately it is hard to avoid in the course of the extremely complicated operations of modern war."

6. This is Meyer's recollection of the conversation, in his chapter "Royan, ville détruite par erreur." Meyer tends to glorify his own activities in this book, but his account fits the other evidence.

7. Three other pieces of evidence support Meyer's claim of German readiness to surrender:

   A. A dispatch in *Samedi-Soir* in May 1948 (reproduced in part in the Botton collection) tells a strange story that goes even further than Meyer. It reports, on the basis of a document it claims to have found in the Ministry of the Armed Forces, that a British agent with the code name of "Aristide," who had parachuted into France to join the Resistance, reported later to his government in London that the Germans in the Royan area had offered to surrender if they would be given the honors of war, but that the French General Bertin said a surrender to the British would create a "diplomatic incident." This was, allegedly, September 8, 1944.

B. An open letter to General de Larminat by Dr. Pierre Veyssière, a former leader of the Royan Resistance (reproduced in the Botton collection), says: "Now we are sure that in August and September, 1944, the German high command—the commander of the fortress of Royan—made proposals of surrender that, if they had come about, would have prevented the worst; we know that on two occasions, he had made contact with Colonel Cominetti, called Charly, commander of the Médoc groups; we know also that these attempts at negotiations were purely and simply repulsed by the French headquarters at Bordeaux, in order, no doubt, to add to the grandeur of military prestige."

C. The article of Paul Métadier (reprinted in a pamphlet, available in the library of Royan) in *La Lettre Médicale*, February 1948, gives Sir Samuel Hoare, former British Ambassador to France, as a source of the fact that the French military command had opposed the surrender of the German general to the British.

8. This story appears also in Robert Aron's *Histoire de la Libération de la France*, June 1944–May 1945 (Librarie Arthème Fayard, 1959). Aron adds the point that the American general spent some time on this visit with an FFI (French Forces of the Interior) journalist who called the inhabitants of Royan "collaborators."

9. Colle, *Royan, son passé, ses environs.* He reports that the Germans, under Admiral Michahelles, had 5,500 men, 150 cannon, and four anti-aircraft batteries. They were well entrenched in concrete bunkers and surrounded by fields of land mines.

10. "*Les Préparatifs de l'Attaque*" in the Botton collection. The same writer claims (on the basis of a historical work by J. Mortin, *Au Carrefour de l'Histoire*) that the formula for napalm was found in the eighteenth century by a Grenoblois goldsmith, who demonstrated it to the minister of war, after which Louis XV was so horrified he ordered the documents burned, saying that such a terrifying force must remain unknown for the good of man.

11. *Revue Historique de l'Armée*, January 1946. An article in a regional journal after the war commented on those engaged in the April attacks: "Thanks to them, one could not say that the French army remained impotent before the German redoubts on the Atlantic wall." *Le Pays d'Ouest*, copy in the library of Royan.

12. Open letter to General de Larminat, caustically addressing him as "Libérateur" de Royan. Reproduced in the Botton collection.

13. The exchange between Métadier and de Larminat is in a pamphlet in the possession of the library in Royan. The original Royan library was destroyed during the bombings, and in 1957, after twelve years, a new library was built.

14. At one point, Meyer quotes Bismarck, who made German students write: "Man was not put in the world to be happy, but to do his duty!" In another frightening glimpse of what a well-trained military man of our century can believe, Meyer talks fondly of that special bond of the sea (*"une commune maîtresse: la mer"*) which unites sailors of different nations in their patriotic duty, as an example of such laudable unity in action, to the landing of European troops in China in 1900 to crush the Boxer uprising.

ABOUT THE AUTHOR

Howard Zinn (August 24, 1922–January 27, 2010) grew up in the immigrant slums of Brooklyn, where he worked in shipyards in his late teens. He saw combat duty as an air force bombardier in World War II and afterward received his doctorate in history from Columbia University and was a postdoctoral Fellow in East Asian Studies at Harvard University. Zinn is the author of many books, including his million-selling classic, *A People's History of the United States*, and *A Power Governments Cannot Suppress*.